Job Quiz

Written by Margaret MacDonald

Picture Dictionary

computer animator

fashion designers

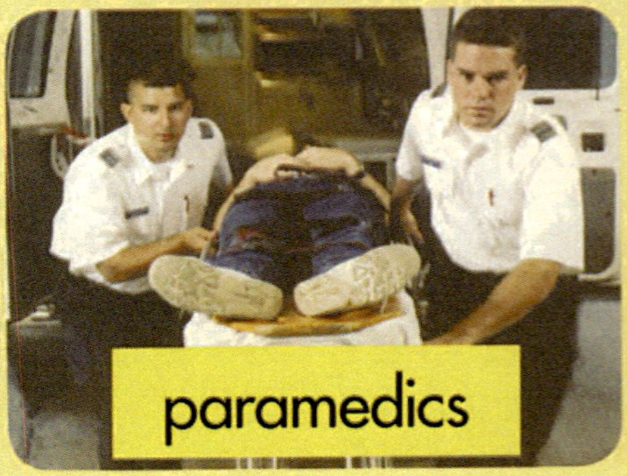
paramedics

potter

scientist

What jobs do the people you know do?
Do you know a teacher?
Do you know a doctor?
Do you know what they do?

What job does this woman do?

I help people who are sick.
I help people who are hurt
in accidents.
I drive an ambulance.
I wear special clothes.
What job do I do?

I am a paramedic.

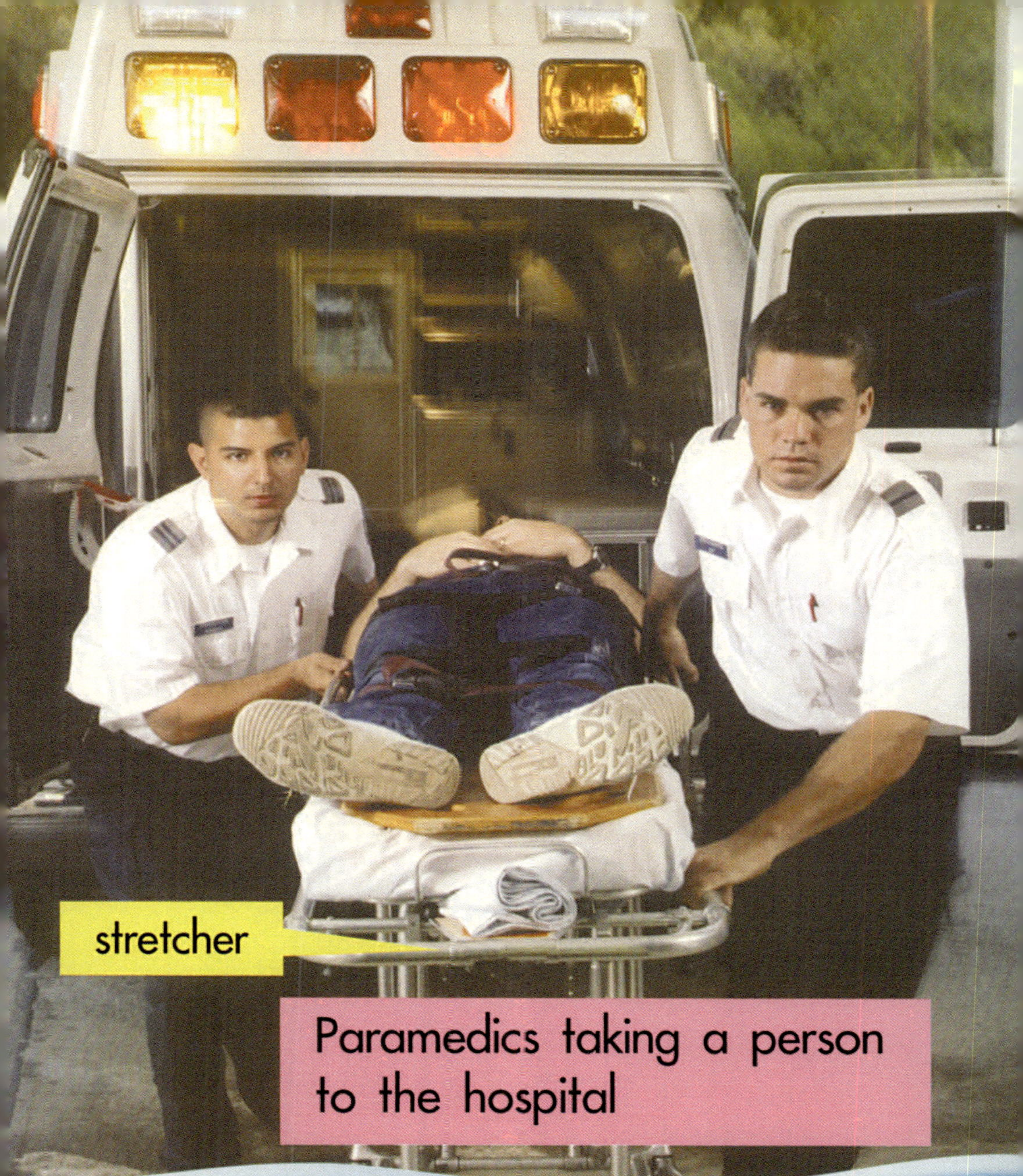

Paramedics taking a person to the hospital

I make things with clay.
I use a wheel
to shape the things I make.
When I have made the shape,
I bake it in a kiln.
What job do I do?

I am a potter.

A potter making a vase

I work in an office.
I use a computer.
I use the computer
to draw pictures.
I make the pictures move.
What job do I do?

I am a computer animator.

A computer animator using the computer to draw a picture

I go to fashion shows
to look at clothes.
I draw pictures of clothes.
People make the clothes
I draw.
What job do I do?

I am a fashion designer.

Fashion designers looking at pictures of clothes

I work in a very cold place.
I study animals that live
in cold places.
What job do I do?

I am a scientist.
I work in Antarctica.

A scientist taking a photo of an emperor penguin

Is My Job Inside or Outside?

Inside Jobs

- Chef
- Computer Animator
- Fashion Designer

Inside and Outside Jobs

- Paramedic
- Potter
- Teacher

Outside Jobs

- Farmer
- Scientist
- Surveyor

chef

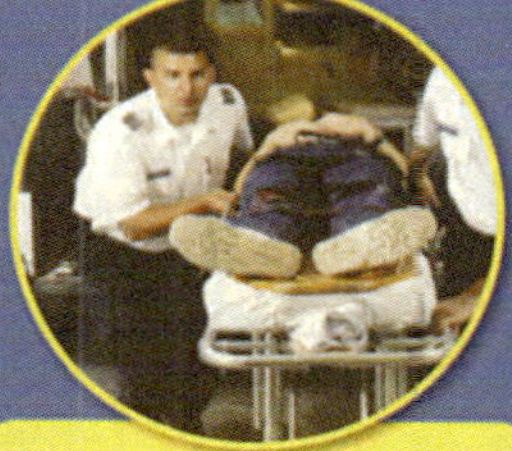

paramedic

farmer

computer animator

potter

scientist

fashion designer

teacher

surveyor

Activity Page

1. Copy this diagram.

2. Write in some more inside and outside jobs you know.

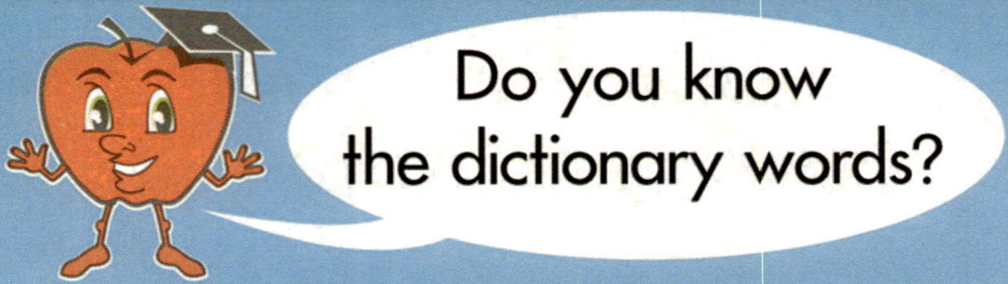